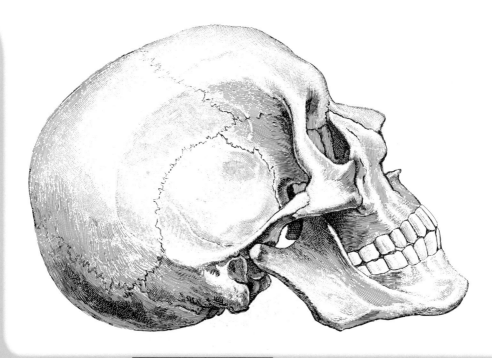

A Timeline of
Medicine

Leeches to
Lasers

WORLD
BOOK

World Book
a Scott Fetzer company
Chicago

WORLD BOOK and the GLOBE DEVICE are registered trademarks or trademarks of World Book, Inc.

World Book, Inc.
180 North LaSalle Street
Suite 900
Chicago, Illinois 60601
USA

For information about other World Book publications, call
1-800-WORLDBK (967-5325).

For information about sales to schools and libraries, call 1-800-975-3250 (United States) or 1-800-837-5365 (Canada).

Produced for World Book, Inc. by Bailey Publishing Associates Ltd.

Library of Congress Cataloging-in-Publication Data

Title: Leeches to lasers: a timeline of medicine.
Description: Chicago: World Book, Inc., a Scott Fetzer company, 2016. | Series: A timeline of... | Includes index.
Identifiers: LCCN 2016012917 | ISBN 9780716635420
Subjects: LCSH: Medicine--History--Juvenile literature. | Medical innovations--History--Juvenile literature.
Classification: LCC R133.5 .L44 2016 | DDC 610.9--dc23
LC record available at https://lccn.loc.gov/2016012917

Leeches to Lasers: A Timeline of Medicine
ISBN: 978-0-7166-3542-0
A Timeline of... Set ISBN: 978-0-7166-3539-0
E-book ISBN: 978-0-7166-3551-2 (ePUB3 format)

Printed in China by Shenzhen Wing King Tong Paper Products Co., Ltd., Guangdong Province
1st printing July 2016

Staff

Writer: Cath Senker

Executive Committee

President
Jim O'Rourke

Vice President and Editor in Chief
Paul A. Kobasa

Vice President, Finance
Donald D. Keller

Vice President, Marketing
Jean Lin

Vice President, International
Kristin Norell

Director, Human Resources
Bev Ecker

Editorial

Manager, Annuals/Series Nonfiction
Christine Sullivan

Editor, Annuals/Series Nonfiction
Kendra Muntz

Manager, Sciences
Jeff De La Rosa

Senior Editor, Sciences
Nick Kilzer

Administrative Assistant Annuals/Series Nonfiction
Ethel Matthews

Manager, Contracts & Compliance (Rights & Permissions)
Loranne K. Shields

Manager, Indexing Services
David Pofelski

Digital

Director, Digital Product Content Development
Emily Kline

Director, Digital Product Development
Erika Meller

Digital Product Manager
Lyndsie Manusos

Digital Product Coordinator
Matthew Werner

Manufacturing/Production

Manufacturing Manager
Sandra Johnson

Production/Technology Manager
Anne Fritzinger

Proofreader
Nathalie Strassheim

Graphics and Design

Senior Art Director
Tom Evans

Senior Designer
Matt Carrington

Media Editor
Rosalia Bledsoe

Manager, Cartographic Services
Wayne K. Pichler

Senior Cartographer
John M. Rejba

Special thanks to:

Roberta Bailey
Nicola Barber
Ian Winton
Alex Woolf

Acknowledgments

Cover photo: Shutterstock (Hein Nouwens).

Bridgeman Picture Library 4 top (Bibliotheque Nationale/Archives Charmet), 10 (Biblioteca Universitaria/Archives Charmet), 11 left, 14 (Archives Charmet).

Corbis 6 (Frederic Soltan), 9 right (Leemage), 17, 18 left, 19, 21 (Heritage Images), 22, 23, 24, 25, 26, 27, 29 left, 30 (Bettmann), 32 left (Hulton-Deutsch Collection), 32 right (Tarker), 33 (Hulton-Deutsch Collection).

Shutterstock 4 bottom (R. Przybysz), 7 left (Andrey_Popov), 8 (Everett Historical), 9 left (P. Krzeslak), 28 (Hein Nouwens), 29 right (BUFOTO), 31 (Everett Historical), 34 (Studio_G), 36 (S. Kaulitzki), 37 (Studio_3321).

Wellcome Library, London 7 right, 11 right, 12, 15, 16 left and right, 18 right (Science Museum, London), 20, 35 (Limbs & Things).

World Book 13.

Glossary There is a glossary of terms on page 38. Terms defined in the glossary are in type that **looks like this** (called *boldface type*) on their first appearance on any *spread* (two facing pages).

Circa Some dates are written with *c.* before the year. The *c.* stands for *circa.* Circa means *approximately.* For example, with c. 250 B.C., the phrase is read as "circa 250 B.C.," meaning *approximately 250 B.C.* Circa can be used with both B.C. and A.D. dates.

Contents

Leeches to Lasers
A Timeline of Medicine

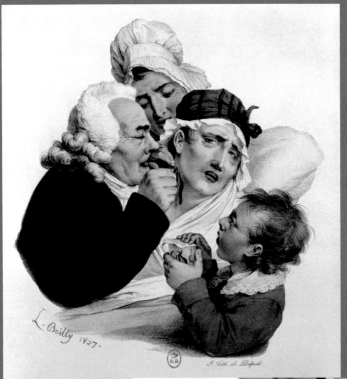

Centuries ago, people frequently used leeches, bloodsucking worms, to help treat illnesses. (Doctors today sometimes use leeches to reduce the pooling of blood in tissues after certain types of surgeries.)

Such modern technology as lasers helps doctors perform difficult surgeries.

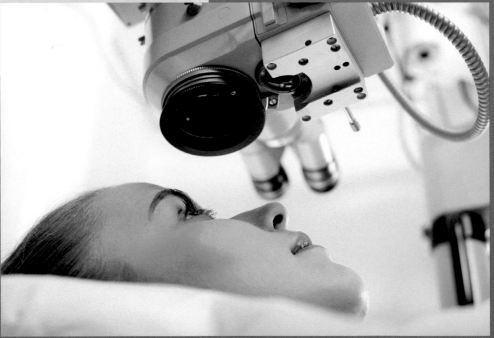

Introduction
Medicine Through the Ages

Throughout history, people have cared for the sick. Medicine has become the science and art of preserving health and treating illness. Medicine is a science because it is based on knowledge gained through study and experimentation. It is an art because its success in curing a sick person depends on how medical professionals apply their knowledge.

Medicine covers many activities, from checking people's overall health to identifying and treating an illness. In the past, healers' treatments included magic spells and religious *rituals* (ceremonies). Today, many people practice medicine, including **midwives,** nurses, doctors, surgeons, and therapists. Sick people may have surgery, take medicines, or see a therapist about mental health concerns.

This book covers some of the great discoveries and inventions in medicine. It explores ancient medical systems, such as the idea that flows of energy through the body could become blocked and cause illness. In the **Middle Ages,** medical schools and hospitals were built. Medicine became a full-time profession. During the 1600's and 1700's, people looked for a scientific basis for medicine rather than relying on ideas from ancient thinkers.

In the 1800's, more people lived in cities where diseases easily spread. The century saw improvements in **hygiene** to prevent disease. **Anesthesia** made surgery painless and **antiseptics** reduced infection. During the 1900's, **vaccinations** prevented many dangerous diseases, and the discovery of the structure of **DNA** opened a path to treat hereditary diseases. Medicine continues to advance as scientists find cures for old and new diseases.

To learn more, follow the timeline through this book to trace the history of medicine and medical practices from the earliest civilizations to the present day.

Chapter 1

The Ancient World
c. 3000 B.C.—c. A.D. 200

In ancient Egypt, India, China, Greece, and Rome, many people believed that good health depended on a person's lifestyle, environment, and the flow of *humors*, or energy, through *channels* that moved through the body. To treat the sick, healers used medicines, traditional cures, simple methods, and prayer. Early healers were not professionally trained. They learned medical practices by following tradition and from their own observations and experiences over time.

Ancient Egyptians developed the first formal system of medicine.

c. 3000 B.C.–1000 B.C.

c. 3000 B.C.

Ayurvedic medicine started in what is now the nation of India. Ayurvedic medicine is a system of care that focuses on a state of overall well-being and balance between physical, emotional, and spiritual parts of a person's life. The ancient Ayurvedic god of medicine was named Lord Dhanvantari.

Ancient Egyptians thought that illness was the result of evil spirits entering the body and blocking its channels. Magic was used to cure the illness. Early medicines were made from foods, plants, shells, herbs, minerals, and animal parts. The Egyptians put honey on wounds to help them heal. Although the Egyptians did not understand how this process worked, scientists now know that honey kills **bacteria** living on a surface. Other ancient medical treatments, however, probably made the illness worse. Egyptian doctors sometimes put soil into a part of the body as a remedy. Rather than help, this method likely hurt the body's natural healing process. But the Egyptians were skilled at setting broken bones. They carried out such basic surgery as stitching serious skin wounds closed.

c. 2500 B.C.

Evidence shows that acupuncture was widely used in areas of what is now the country of China. Acupuncture is the ancient practice of inserting needles into the body to relieve pain and illness.

c. 1550 B.C.

The Ebers Papyrus, an ancient Egyptian medical text, was written around 1550 B.C. It is one of the oldest medical documents ever discovered. It describes blood vessels in the human body and lists over 700 home remedies and magic formulas to cure sickness.

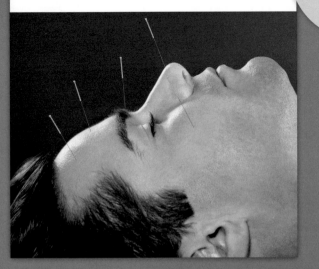

c. 1000 B.C.

Ayurvedic doctors in what is now India developed surgical techniques to treat many injuries and conditions. They used about 125 surgical instruments. They invented plastic surgery techniques to replace damaged noses and ears.

The Ancient World
c. 3000 B.C.—c. A.D. 200

Around 100 B.C., texts describing ancient Chinese traditional medicine were written down. Chinese healers believed that two opposing forces in the body, *yin* and *yang*, had to be kept in balance for good health. For treatment, healers used acupuncture and medicines made from plants that had been discovered many centuries earlier.

In ancient Greece and Rome, the focus of medicine was keeping the body healthy. Fitness and **hygiene** were important. The Greeks used gymnasiums and swimming pools to exercise. Ancient Romans maintained hygiene by using public baths

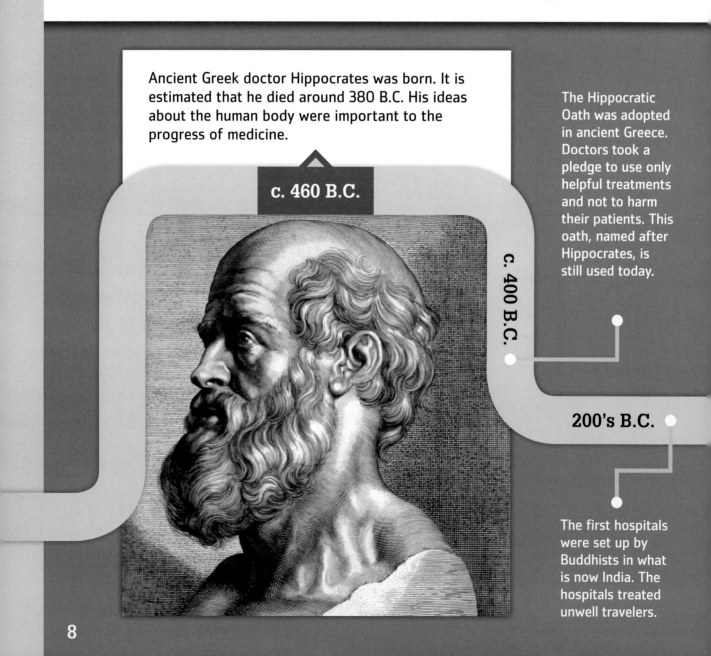

Ancient Greek doctor Hippocrates was born. It is estimated that he died around 380 B.C. His ideas about the human body were important to the progress of medicine.

c. 460 B.C.

c. 400 B.C.

The Hippocratic Oath was adopted in ancient Greece. Doctors took a pledge to use only helpful treatments and not to harm their patients. This oath, named after Hippocrates, is still used today.

200's B.C.

The first hospitals were set up by Buddhists in what is now India. The hospitals treated unwell travelers.

and toilets and by drinking clean water from *aqueducts* (channels built to carry water). Greek doctor Hippocrates believed the body contained four bodily fluids called *humors.* These humors were blood, black bile, yellow bile, and phlegm. He thought that the four humors were well balanced in a healthy person. But any bodily imbalance of the humors led to disease. For example, Hippocrates thought that too much blood in a person's body caused fever. To correct this, doctors once commonly used what they called *medicinal leeches*. A leech is a type of worm. When used in medicine, the animal clings to a person's body and sucks out blood. Although today's doctors follow different methods, Hippocrates's ideas influenced people who practiced medicine for many centuries.

The foundations of Chinese traditional medicine were compiled. They were based on the book *Yellow Emperor's Inner Canon,* which brought together knowledge about health and disease gathered over thousands of years. (A *canon* is a set of rules.) The book described *yin* and *yang*. Yin was thought to be dark, cool, and female. Yang was bright, warm, and male. Yin and yang were believed to affect every person's health.

c. A.D. 129–c. A.D. 200

Ancient Greek doctor Galen (c. A.D. 129- c. A.D. 200) used a new method to study the body. He *dissected* (cut apart) the bodies of dead animals to learn about their internal parts. He found that the arteries contain blood, but he did not fully understand how blood moved through the body. Around A.D. 157 he became a doctor for *gladiators* (professional fighters). This position allowed him to study the internal organs and muscles of wounded men. Galen promoted the theory of the four humors. Though some of his ideas were later disproved, his work influenced doctors until the 1800's.

c. 100 B.C.

Chapter 2

Medicine in the Middle Ages
A.D. 300's—1350's

In the **Middle Ages,** also called the *medieval period,* **Muslim** scholars translated ancient Greek medical texts into Arabic and then Latin, the language of educated Europeans. Through these translations, the theory of the four humors spread throughout Europe. It was adopted by many European healers and doctors. Other people believed that illness was a punishment for sinful behavior. In Western and Eastern countries, people of faith cared for the physical and spiritual lives of the

The first accurate description of leprosy, an infectious disease, appeared in copies of writings by the Indian physician Sushruta. He lived almost 1,000 years earlier.

The School of Salerno was the first European medical school. It was built in what is now Italy. The school became the main center of medical learning in the 1000's and 1100's.

c. A.D. 900

A.D. 300's   A.D. 700's

A smallpox **epidemic** swept through North Africa and southern Europe. Smallpox caused a rash that turned into *pustules* (pimples filled with pus), which scabbed over and left scars. The disease scarred, blinded, and killed many people.

sick in such religious communities as monasteries. In these places, prayer was believed to be an important method to help heal the sick.

During the 1100's, some areas of Europe were under Muslim rule. In these areas, several new hospitals were built. Medical schools were also established at new universities. Both the hospitals and schools improved overall healthcare for people in Europe. Over time, medicine became accepted as a serious and important profession. Doctors who had trained at medical schools were considered the top experts. Barber-surgeons, people who both cut hair and performed surgeries, filled the next highest medical position. Nurses and **midwives** working in hospitals and monasteries followed. Apothecaries prepared and sold medicines and gave general health advice.

Al-Rāzī (A.D. 865–A.D. 925?), a Persian doctor, clearly described measles and smallpox in his pioneering medical books and manuscripts.

c. A.D. 900

Working in what is now Spain, Muslim surgeon Abu al-Qasim al-Zahrawi (A.D. 936-1013) completed his 30-volume medical encyclopedia, *The Method*. These books were the first illustrated works about surgeries. They included drawings of more than 200 surgical instruments, or tools. The books were translated into Latin in the 1100's, and Al-Zahrawi's name was given as Albucasis. This translation became the most important surgery textbook in Europe for over 500 years.

c. A.D. 1000

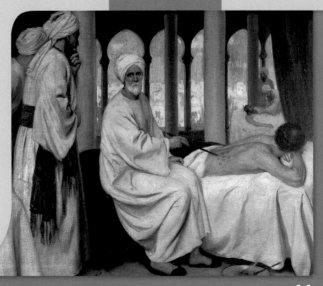

Medicine in the Middle Ages
A.D. 300's—1350's

In the early years of medicine, little attention was given to mental health. It took a long time before people studied the human mind as much as the human body. Instead, many doctors focused on the four humors theory. They thought that to cure any sickness, bad substances needed to be removed from inside the body. Doctors sometimes gave patients medicines to make them vomit or cut patients' bodies to allow them to bleed. In a common method called *cupping,* a doctor put a piece of burning cloth inside a bell-shaped cup. The cup was placed over an open cut in the skin. The suction of the cup drew blood out of the cut. Like ancient healers, European doctors also used medicinal leeches to suck blood out of a body. However, extreme bleeding often made the patient weaker.

c. 1000

Persian doctor Ibn-Sina (A.D. 980-1037) wrote a five-volume encyclopedia titled *Canon of Medicine*. His books brought together all of the knowledge about medicines and the human body known at this time. Ibn-Sina described how herbs could be used for treatment. He also explained how to treat *tumors* (growths), wounds, broken bones, bites, poisoning, and more. *Canon of Medicine* was translated into Latin in the 1100's. These books were used as medical texts for over 600 years. Ibn-Sina is also known as Avicenna.

Hospital building increased in Europe.

1100's

European doctors also treated many diseases with *herbal remedies* (medicines made from plants), along with charms and prayers that they believed would speed up the healing process. Medieval barber-surgeons set broken bones, removed bladder stones, and *amputated* (cut off) limbs. Surgery was both extremely painful and dangerous because of the high risk of infection.

Such **epidemics** as leprosy, plague, and smallpox were major health hazards. At this time, there was no cure for these terrible diseases. People avoided plague victims by painting crosses on the victims' houses. The cross warned others to keep away so they did not catch and spread the disease. Some people also forced those with leprosy to live in separate communities.

Leprosy became an epidemic in Europe. This infectious disease affected the skin and damaged feet and hands. Victims did not usually die but were horribly disabled. Their appearance was sometimes frightening.

Spread of plague in:
1347
1348
1349
1350
1351
1352

1347–1352

1100's–1200's

The Black Death plague traveled through much of Europe and Asia. Initially spread by infected fleas, one form of this disease caused painful swelling in the armpits, legs, or neck. It quickly killed its victims. By 1400, up to 40 percent of the population of Europe—around 25 million people—had lost their lives to this plague.

13

Chapter 3

The Renaissance
Late 1300's—1600's

The **Renaissance** was a period in European history from about the 1300's to the 1600's when the study of medicine and other sciences, art, literature, and history gained new significance. Many factors contributed to the increased scientific study of the human body during the Renaissance. In the mid-1400's, German inventor Johannes Gutenberg created the printing press in Europe. This invention allowed books to be printed by machines instead of copied by hand. Inexpensive printed books helped to spread ideas and information about medicine and many

Italian hospitals began to give free medical care to the sick. *Nuns* (women living in religious communities) and nurses often worked at the hospitals.

Mid-1400's

Late 1400's

German Johannes Gutenberg (1395?-1468?) invented the printing press. By 1500, millions of books on many topics, including medicine, had been printed.

other topics to thousands of people. Rather than rely on knowledge from ancient doctors, Renaissance scientists performed experiments to learn about the human body and disease. Swiss doctor Philippus Paracelsus (1493-1541) challenged the old idea that an imbalance of the four humors caused disease. He thought that each disease had its own particular cause. Paracelsus's work helped to disprove the ideas about the connection between health and the humors.

During this period, universities and hospitals continued to be built. Learning about **anatomy** also improved medical treatments. Such Renaissance artists as Leonardo da Vinci (1452-1519) and Michelangelo (1475-1564) dissected, or cut apart, bodies of people who had died to learn more about how the human body systems work. Da Vinci recorded his studies on human anatomy in more than 750 drawings.

French army doctor Ambroise Paré (1510-1590) is considered the father of modern surgery. He greatly improved surgical techniques. Paré opposed the common practice of cauterizing, or burning, wounds with boiling oil to prevent infection. Instead, he developed the much more effective method of applying a mild ointment, or cream, and then allowing the wound to heal naturally.

c. 1500's

1543

Andreas Vesalius (1514-1564), a professor of medicine in Italy, wrote the first textbook on human anatomy, titled *On the Structure of the Human Body*. This book showed that many of the ancient ideas about anatomy were wrong. Vesalius stated that the heart had four *chambers* (sections) and not three, as the ancient Greek doctor Galen had thought.

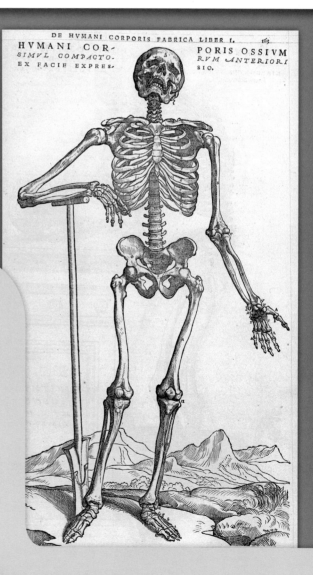

DE HVMANI CORPORIS FABRICA LIBER I. 163
HVMANI COR-
SIMVL COMPACTO.
EX FACIE EXPRES.
PORIS OSSIVM
RVM ANTERIORI
SIO.

The Renaissance
Late 1300's—1600's

Beginning about 1300, European universities held **anatomy** demonstrations and lectures for medical students. Nurses and **midwives** oversaw childbirth and helped care for babies. Some **Renaissance** midwives studied to become trusted medical experts. More and more people began to see the body as a complex structure that needed constant study and experimentation to better understand its function. Over time, the more knowledge medical experts gained about the body, the better they were able to help cure infections and illnesses.

Travel for trade and settlement also became more common. As people traveled,

English doctor William Harvey (1578-1657) published *An Anatomical Study of the Motion of the Heart and of the Blood in Animals.* The study showed that the human heart works like a pump, pushing blood through pathways called *arteries* and around the body. He found that the blood flowed back to the heart through another set of pathways called *veins*.

1628

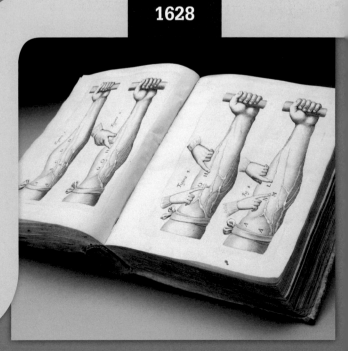

Dutch eyeglass-maker Zacharias Janssen (c. 1585-c. 1638) discovered the principle of the compound microscope. Because Janssen was still a youth at the time, his father likely provided much help. A compound microscope uses a set of lenses that work together to *magnify* (increase in size) an image. This device allowed scientists to study **cells** in detail.

c. 1590

they carried diseases to different parts of the world. For example, in the early 1500's, Spanish settlers from Europe brought smallpox to the Americas. Smallpox was not usually fatal to Europeans. But because North and South American native peoples had never been exposed to smallpox, this disease killed millions of them. As Africans were forcibly shipped to the Americas to work as slaves, they carried such diseases as malaria and yellow fever to new populations in the Americas.

As diseases spread across the world, treatments for those diseases followed. New medicines were exchanged among peoples from Africa, Asia, Europe, the Middle East, and North and South America. Despite new treatments, many people still relied on traditional herbal remedies, prayers, and rituals to manage their health.

Quinine was developed to treat malaria. Cinchona, a tree from what is now Peru, contains quinine in its bark. This medicine did not provide a complete cure, but it remained the only treatment for malaria until the mid-1940's.

1630's   **1665**

English scientist Robert Hooke (1653-1703) used an early microscope to discover plant cells in a slice of cork. He named the structures "cells" because they looked like little walled rooms.

1671

1674

English midwife Jane Sharp (1641?-1671?) wrote *The Midwives Book*, which gave details about **anatomy,** pregnancy, birth, and caring for babies.

Anton van Leeuwenhoek (1632-1723), a Dutch scientist, was one of the first people to record observations of microscopic, or tiny, **bacteria.**

Chapter 4

Enlightenment Medical Thought
1700's—Early 1800's

The **Enlightenment** was a time in Europe from the 1600's to the late 1700's when people began to challenge long-held ideas and beliefs about many subjects. The leaders of the Enlightenment relied heavily on the scientific method, with its emphasis on experimentation and careful observation. In medicine, scientists and doctors moved away from the idea that sinful behaviors caused disease. They started to view the body as a machine with organs that worked according

For many centuries, Turkish, Chinese, and Arab healers protected people from smallpox by **inoculating** them with the disease. After inoculation, many people developed a mild case of smallpox and then became **immune** from the disease forever. In 1717, English writer Lady Mary Wortley Montagu (1689-1762) saw this method on a trip to Turkey and had her children inoculated. She later promoted the method in England, where it was thought to be dangerous.

The London Foundling Hospital for orphaned babies opened.

1741

1745

In Britain, the jobs of barber and surgeon were separated. The practice of surgery became a professional career. Surgeons used many special tools.

1717

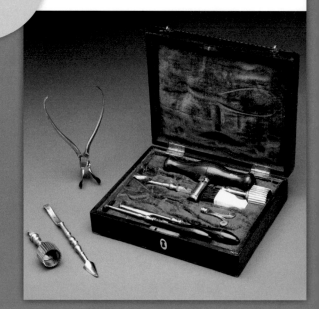

to the laws of nature. A greater knowledge of **anatomy** improved the success of sometimes dangerous surgeries. Scientists began to perform *autopsies* on the dead. An autopsy is a careful examination of both the outside and inside of a dead body to find the cause of death. Today, autopsies are one of the top methods for finding or better understanding a person's cause of death.

Education and training for doctors and surgeons greatly improved in the 1700's. Medical societies were set up, special medical journals were printed, and new rules were made to ensure doctors and surgeons were properly trained. In about 1750, hospitals were common across much of Europe and North America. Charities and wealthy people often paid for the hospitals to be built. Specialty hospitals meant for groups of people suffering from similar illnesses were also built.

Mid-1700's

Separate hospitals called *asylums* were built in Europe for people with mental illnesses.

1747

Scottish doctor James Lind (1716-1794) studied scurvy, a disease that causes weakness, bleeding of the gums, and *hemorrhages* (bleeding in the body). Sailors often suffered from scurvy. Lind gave sailors oranges and lemons to eat, which cured the disease. Many years later, doctors found that a lack of vitamin C in the body causes scurvy. Because citrus fruits, juices, and many vegetables contain large amounts of this vitamin, eating these foods can prevent and cure this disease.

Enlightenment Medical Thought

1700's—Early 1800's

In Europe during the **Enlightenment,** mental illnesses were called by such names as *melancholy* and *mania*. Little was done to help people who had these types of illnesses. Some people believed that mental illness was caused by mystical forces. More women were diagnosed with mania than men. It was thought that pregnancy and childbirth could change women's mental states.

Those who suffered from mental problems were feared and thought to be a danger to society. They were sometimes sent to special hospitals called *asylums.* The conditions in asylums were often cruel. There was little professional care to

1761

1795

Italian scientist Giovanni Battista Morgagni (1682-1771) published a book called *On the Seats and Causes of Diseases*. This book showed that disease often resulted when a particular organ of the body is not working correctly. Morgagni's work marked an important breakthrough in a branch of medicine called *pathology*—the study of disease.

Philippe Pinel of France (1745-1826) and William Tuke of England (1732-1822) worked to improve the conditions of mental institutions in their countries. They fought for more humane treatment of patients. Through their efforts, many mental hospitals introduced treatment programs that included fresh air and pleasant surroundings.

help people get well. But in the late 1700's, efforts to improve the conditions of mental institutions in Europe gained more attention in society.

People in what is now China and other Asian countries better understood the close relationship between the mind and body in shaping mental health. Doctors in these regions looked at a person's physical, mental, and spiritual well being together rather than only charting their physical symptoms. In China, doctors believed mental health was linked with the life forces of *yin* and *yang,* just like bodily health. They treated mental illnesses in the same way as physical problems, with such methods as acupuncture and herbal remedies.

1796

English physician Edward Jenner (1749-1823) developed a method of **vaccination** to protect people from getting smallpox. Jenner took infected matter from the hand of a local dairymaid who had cowpox. He inserted the material into small cuts on the arm of a healthy eight-year-old boy. After 48 days, Jenner injected the boy with smallpox, but the boy did not become ill. The boy had become **immune** to smallpox. This was the first vaccination ever given.

1798

The Lying-In Hospital of the City of New York was founded for pregnant women.

1813

Surgeons in Britain were required to have at least one year of experience working in a hospital to be allowed to practice surgery.

Chapter 5

The Industrial Revolution
Mid-1800's

The late 1700's and early 1800's is a period of time known as the Industrial Revolution. The Industrial Revolution began in Britain, then spread across Europe, the United States, and later, Australia. The Industrial Revolution created an enormous increase in the production of such goods as cloth and iron. The development of steam engines helped to power many types of machines used to make and transport goods. Factories were built to house the machines. Canal boats, and later trains, transported raw materials and products for sale.

William T. G. Morton (1819-1868), an American dentist, publicly demonstrated the use of ether, a liquid that causes unconsciousness when its vapor is breathed in. Ether was used during surgeries for the next 100 years.

1842

1846

1847

British lawyer Edwin Chadwick (1800-1890) wrote a report called *The Sanitary Condition of the Labouring Population of Great Britain*. This report linked poor **sanitary** conditions in Britain with the spread of diseases.

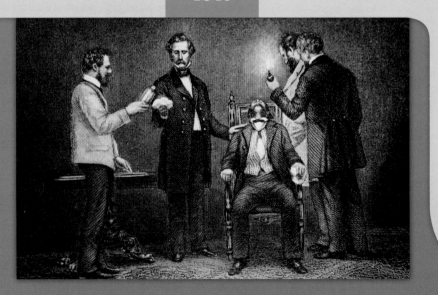

Hungarian doctor Ignaz Semmelweis (1827-1912), working in Vienna, Austria, advised doctors to wash their hands before delivering babies. By washing their hands before and after caring for patients, doctors were less likely to spread disease from one person to another. This simple act dramatically cut the newborn death rate from infection. Semmelweis's ideas were not widely accepted until British surgeon Sir Joseph Lister (1827-1912) proved his ideas correct in 1865.

Thousands of people moved to large cities to work in the new factories. They lived in overcrowded buildings without clean water or sewage systems. The coal-burning factories polluted, or dirtied, the air. Workers labored long hours in filthy conditions. Diseases easily spread in the crowded homes and factories. Many people suffered accidents in the factories. Some developed lung disease from working in coal mines. Such dangerous **epidemics** as smallpox, yellow fever, cholera, typhoid, and typhus affected the health of thousands of people.

During the 1800's, laws to improve public health and **hygiene** were introduced. In Britain, the Public Health Act of 1848 was the first step in improving **sanitation,** or cleanliness. The act also called for examinations of foods that were for sale. In the United States, such rapidly growing cities as New York began to improve sanitation.

The Shattuck report, published by the Massachusetts Sanitary Commission, studied the serious public health problems in Boston, Massachusetts, in the United States.

1848

1850

The British government passed the Public Health Act of 1848. This act established a Central Board of Health. It also encouraged local governments to improve public health by providing clean water supplies and disposing of waste.

The Industrial Revolution
Mid-1800's

Throughout the 1800's, scientists developed safer anesthetics. Anesthetics make patients unconscious during surgery so they do not feel pain. This special medicine is called **anesthesia.** Japanese surgeon Hanaoka Seishu (1760-1835) made his anesthesia using a mixture of herbs and some of the substances used in anesthetics today. In the United States in the 1840's, dentists experimented with giving patients ether and nitrous oxide, commonly known as *laughing gas.* Ether is a colorless liquid that causes unconsciousness when its vapor is inhaled. American doctor Crawford W. Long (1815-1878) used ether during surgery as early as 1842. Using anesthetics also gave surgeons more time to carry out difficult operations

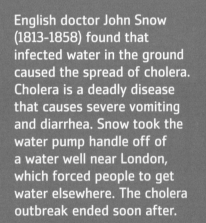

English doctor John Snow (1813-1858) found that infected water in the ground caused the spread of cholera. Cholera is a deadly disease that causes severe vomiting and diarrhea. Snow took the water pump handle off of a water well near London, which forced people to get water elsewhere. The cholera outbreak ended soon after.

1853–1854

1854

English nurse Florence Nightingale (1820-1910) arrived in what is now Ukraine. Six years later, in 1860, she founded the Nightingale Training School for Nurses at St. Thomas's Hospital in London, England.

on the abdomen, head, and chest. Before the development of safe anesthesia, these operations would have taken too long and been too painful for the patient to survive.

As nursing slowly became a more accepted medical profession for women, hospital care greatly improved. The events of the Crimean War (1853–1856) showed the importance of skilled nurses. In 1854, English nurse Florence Nightingale took charge of the war hospital for British troops in what is now Ukraine. She organized a detailed cleaning of the building and set up a nursing schedule for patient care and daily work. Doctors and army officials came to respect her leadership. Jamaican nurse Mary Grant Seacole (1805-1881) also provided care for wounded British soldiers near the front line in war battles.

1857

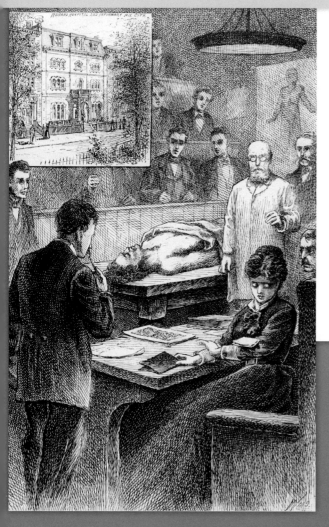

Elizabeth Blackwell (1821-1910) was the first professional woman doctor in the United States. She entered Geneva Medical School in New York in 1847, after 29 schools had refused to accept a female student. In 1857, she and her surgeon sister, Emily, opened a hospital in New York City. The hospital, called the New York Infirmary for Women and Children, was staffed entirely by women. It primarily served the poor. In 1868, the Blackwell sisters founded a women's medical school at the hospital. By the late 1800's, there were seven medical schools for women in the U.S.

1858

German scientist Rudolf Virchow (1821-1902) wrote the book *Cellular Pathology*. He explained that diseases occur within an organ's individual **cells,** not in the organ as a whole. Virchow helped to develop pathology, the study of disease.

Chapter 6

New Developments in Medicine
Late 1800's

In the 1800's, French scientist Louis Pasteur continued studying English physician Edward Jenner's work on **vaccination** from the late 1700's. Pasteur proved that such **germs** as **bacteria** and **viruses** multiply in the body and can cause disease. He also found that every kind of disease has its own type of germ. Pasteur experimented with germs in a laboratory. He weakened germs that cause a particular disease and then placed the germs into an animal's body. He found that the animal developed **immunity** to that particular disease. This means that the animal will not become sick if the same germs enter its body again in the future.

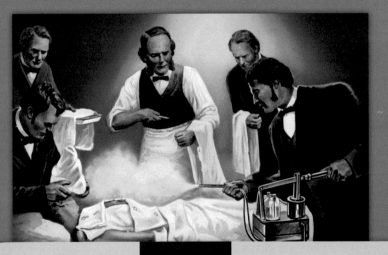

The Board of Health in New York City was the first public health organization established in the United States. In Britain, the Sanitary Act of 1866 required local governments to clean streets, maintain sewers, and check the water supply for bacteria.

1865

1866

1877

British surgeon Sir Joseph Lister (1827-1912) was the first person to use **antiseptics** during surgery. Lister's groundbreaking technique greatly reduced the number of patients who died from infection after having surgery.

French scientist Louis Pasteur (1822-1895) produced a **vaccine** that prevented anthrax, a disease that killed farm animals.

Pasteur's important discovery was the start of finding new medicines to treat each specific disease.

In the 1850's, Pasteur also learned about germs by studying the production of beer, wine, and milk. He showed that germs make food decay, or go bad, but that heat could kill the germs. The method of heating substances to kill germs is called *pasteurization,* named after Pasteur.

German physician Robert Koch discovered the bacteria responsible for the diseases anthrax, tuberculosis, and cholera. Other scientists followed Koch's method for identifying germs to find the causes of the tropical diseases malaria, yellow fever, and sleeping sickness.

Robert Koch (1843-1910), a German physician, showed that a certain type of bacteria caused a particular disease. Koch created a four-step method to study bacteria. These steps are famously known as *Koch's Postulates.*

Koch's Postulates are:

1. Scientists take bacteria from sick animals that cause disease.

2. Scientists grow the bacteria in a laboratory.

3. Scientists inject the bacteria into animals.

4. Scientists take bacteria from the diseased animals and check they are the same kind as the original bacteria.

1877

1882

Koch discovered the bacteria responsible for the disease tuberculosis.

New Developments in Medicine
Late 1800's

Fellow German scientist Paul Ehrlich (1854-1915) worked with Robert Koch on tuberculosis **bacteria.** They discovered that certain chemicals that were used as dyes could also cure some diseases common in such tropical climates as the islands in the Caribbean Sea. In the late 1800's and early 1900's, schools of tropical medicine were set up in Australia, Europe, and the United States.

In the mid-1800's, doctors started to use **antiseptics** to kill **germs** that caused infection. Beginning in the 1860's, British surgeon Sir Joseph Lister introduced sprays called *antiseptics* that killed the germs in the air, on the surgeon's hands,

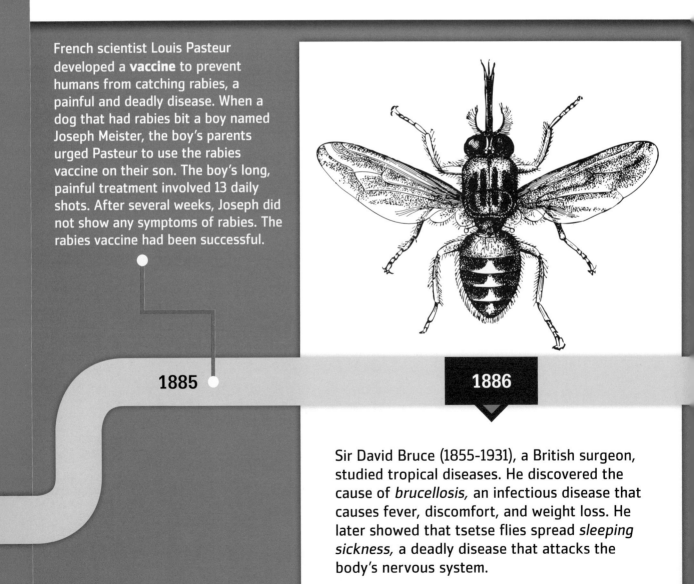

French scientist Louis Pasteur developed a **vaccine** to prevent humans from catching rabies, a painful and deadly disease. When a dog that had rabies bit a boy named Joseph Meister, the boy's parents urged Pasteur to use the rabies vaccine on their son. The boy's long, painful treatment involved 13 daily shots. After several weeks, Joseph did not show any symptoms of rabies. The rabies vaccine had been successful.

1885

1886

Sir David Bruce (1855-1931), a British surgeon, studied tropical diseases. He discovered the cause of *brucellosis,* an infectious disease that causes fever, discomfort, and weight loss. He later showed that tsetse flies spread *sleeping sickness,* a deadly disease that attacks the body's nervous system.

on surgical instruments, on bandages, and on the patient's skin. Applying antiseptics before and after surgery greatly reduced the chance of a patient developing an infection after surgery.

Lister's method came to be called *aseptic surgery*. This technique involved keeping germs away from surgical wounds from the start by sterilizing the equipment in the operating areas. Sterilizing is the process of killing the germs in or on an object. Surgeons sterilized equipment and clothing before surgery. Doctors began wearing clean white coats, masks, and gloves. Before such new developments in medicine, a patient's risk of death by infection after surgery was high. But by the end of the 1800's, many patients had an increased chance of surviving surgery.

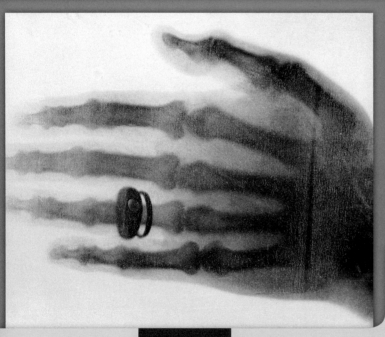

X rays were first used on wounded soldiers to find bullets and *shrapnel*—small pieces of metal thrown out of an exploding bomb that became stuck deep inside the body.

1896

1898

British doctor Sir Ronald Ross (1857-1932) proved that mosquitoes can carry and spread malaria.

1895

German scientist Wilhelm Conrad Roentgen (1845-1923) created the first **X-ray** image. X rays allow people to see inside the body. For this discovery, he won the first Nobel Prize in physics in 1901. In the early 1900's, X-ray machines were put into hospitals. They were first used to spot *tumors,* or growths, and to screen for tuberculosis. But, the power of X rays proved dangerous in large doses.

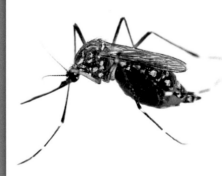

Chapter 7

How Modern Wars Affected Medicine
1900—1948

In the early 1900's, deadly new weapons were developed. By World War I (1914–1918), machine guns could fire hundreds of shots in under a minute. There were huge *artillery weapons* (heavy guns), poison gas, and flame-throwers that shot out burning fuel. Doctors had to learn to treat patients with severe war injuries. Preventing infection was important. Nurses used a special lotion to clean wounds and then wrapped the wounds in gauze, or cloth, soaked in the same lotion.

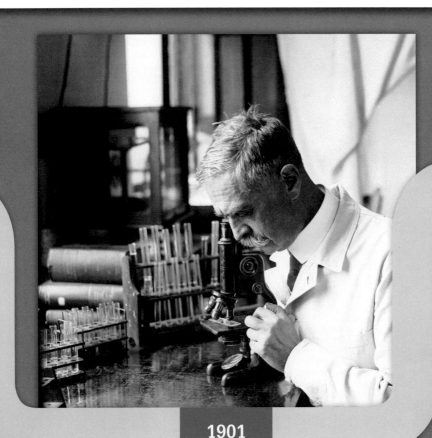

World War I caused great loss of life and left huge numbers of people injured or disabled around the world.

1914–1918   **1917**

A mental illness called *shell shock* was identified. Many soldiers developed this illness after they came home from war. People with the disorder repeatedly remember, relive, or dream about a terrible experience. Today, this psychological disorder is called *Post-Traumatic Stress Disorder,* or *PTSD.*

1901

Karl Landsteiner (1868-1943), an Austrian-American scientist, discovered three major human blood types, A, B, and O. In 1902, he discovered blood type AB.

Sometimes soldiers' injuries could not be seen on the outside of the body. **X-ray** machines were used to detect injuries suffered on the inside of the body. Polish-born French scientist Marie Skłodowska Curie (1867-1934) worked for the Red Cross, an organization whose members work to relieve human suffering. She brought X-ray machines close to the war's front lines to better treat patients.

Wounded people often needed a *blood transfusion* (the transfer of an amount of another person's blood into a wounded person's bloodstream). But blood transfusions during this time often made the patient even sicker. Austrian-American scientist Karl Landsteiner discovered that people have different blood types. Using the wounded person's correct blood type during a blood transfusion made the process much safer and more successful.

A global **epidemic** of influenza, called the Spanish flu, killed 20 to 50 million people worldwide. Many soldiers died of influenza. Wartime troop movements may have helped spread the disease.

1917

1918-1919

Sir Harold Gillies (1882-1960), a surgeon from New Zealand, improved plastic surgery. He used new methods to repair the skin of soldiers damaged by horrific war wounds and burns. He took skin from an unharmed part of the body and moved it to the injured area.

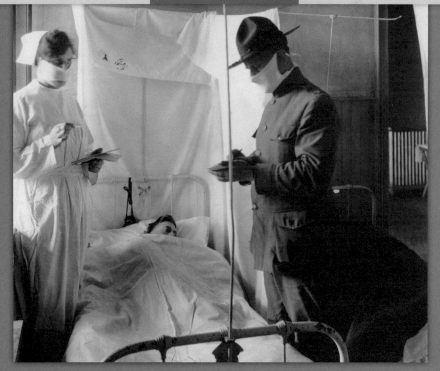

How Modern Wars Affected Medicine
1900—1948

In 1922, Canadian surgeon Sir Frederick Grant Banting and his assistant, Charles Best (1899-1978), published their discovery of a **hormone** called *insulin.* Banting and Best worked in a laboratory provided by Toronto Professor John James Rickard Macleod. The body produces insulin to control the amount of sugar in the bloodstream. Some people's bodies do not produce enough insulin, causing them to develop a disease called *diabetes.* The complications of diabetes can include heart disease and kidney problems. Until the 1920's, there was no treatment for diabetes. But by 1923, insulin from cows was made available to treat humans. This medicine allowed people with diabetes to help manage their blood sugar levels.

Sir Frederick Grant Banting (1891-1941), a Canadian surgeon, won the Nobel prize in medicine, together with Professor John James Rickard Macleod (1876-1935), for the discovery of insulin.

1923

1928

British doctor Sir Alexander Fleming (1881-1955) discovered penicillin.

In 1928, British doctor Sir Alexander Fleming discovered penicillin, a mold that kills **bacteria.** Penicillin was used to create the world's first **antibiotic** medicine. This life-saving medicine allowed doctors to treat serious infections caused by bacteria. Since this discovery, scientists have made hundreds of other antibiotics, including streptomycin, which helps to treat many diseases. During World War II (1939-1945), thousands of medical workers used penicillin to treat the wounded.

In 1948, the World Health Organization (WHO) was formed to promote health worldwide and address global health problems. Its goals were to prevent disease, provide safe drinking water, maintain sewage systems, and provide **vaccinations** to protect against childhood diseases.

Beginning in 1938, British biochemists Ernst Chain (1906-1979) and Howard Florey (1898-1968) worked to purify penicillin in a way that made it usable as an antibiotic.

American scientist Selman Waksman (1888-1973) developed the antibiotic called *streptomycin* from a mold that is found in soil. Streptomycin helps to treat tuberculosis, pneumonia, and infections of the urinary system.

1938

1948

1929

The first health insurance plan was introduced in the United States. People prepaid money into the health plan to pay for services when they needed medical care.

Chapter 8

Medicine Today
1948—Today

Since World War II (1939-1945), *preventive medicine* (treatment that helps protect against illness) has greatly improved. The use of **vaccines** has saved millions of lives around the world. For example, the current worldwide effort in support of the poliomyelitis, or polio, vaccine has almost completely eliminated the disease. Polio can cause people to lose the use of their limbs or the muscles that control breathing. Before the vaccine was invented in the 1950's, polio was a common threat. But by 2015, only three countries reported cases of polio.

British biologist Francis Crick (1916-2004) and American biologist James Watson (1931-) discovered the structure of DNA, the basis of **heredity.**

American researcher Jonas Salk (1914-1995) developed an effective polio vaccine. An improved *oral* (to be swallowed) version was invented by Albert B. Sabin (1906-1993) in the 1960's.

1948   **1953**   **1954**

1960's

The British government set up the National Health Service to provide medical care to all citizens. This system was based on medical need.

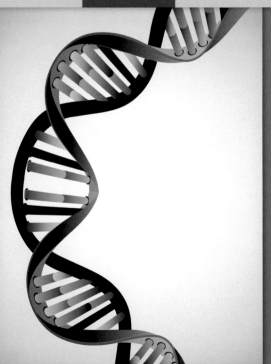

Oral contraceptives, medicine that women can take to stop them from becoming pregnant, became available in the United States. During the 1960's, this medication was introduced in many countries, including Australia, Canada, and Britain.

In 1953, British biologist Francis Crick and American biologist James Watson discovered the structure of **DNA,** with the help of other scientists. DNA, short for *deoxyribonucleic acid*, makes up all of the **genes** that are passed down from parent to child. Genes determine the development of living things, deciding such features as height and hair color. During the 1970's, scientists learned how to change the genes of **bacteria** to make such human **hormones** as insulin, used for treating diabetes.

New discoveries surrounding mental health illnesses have changed treatment methods. New medicines allow sufferers to live in the community instead of in separate hospitals. Many therapy and counseling programs are available for those with psychological illness. Modern treatment methods can help people recover from their symptoms more quickly than in the past.

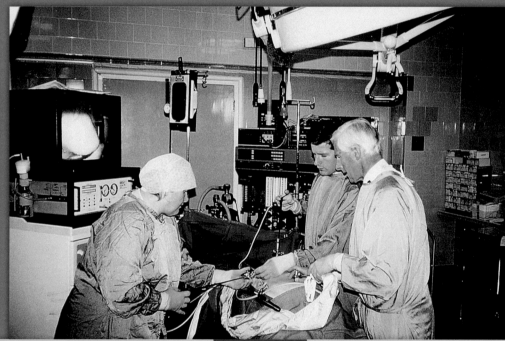

South African surgeon Christiaan Barnard (1922-2001) carried out the first human heart transplant in Cape Town, South Africa.

1967

1980

Laparoscopic surgery, also called *minimally invasive* or *keyhole* surgery, was introduced to the operating room. In this type of procedure, a surgeon makes a small hole in the body and inserts a tiny tube with a light and a video camera. This camera allows the doctor to see inside the body while operating. It helps the doctor fix the correct body part and allows patients to heal more quickly from surgery.

Medicine Today

1948—Today

Major advances in surgery have allowed surgeons to use new techniques on patients. The surgical method called *microsurgery* is less risky for patients than regular surgery. In microsurgery, surgeons look through a microscope while using tiny instruments to carry out complicated operations. Doctors also use lasers, or powerful beams of light, to treat skin disorders, improve eyesight, and shatter gallstones. Precise laser beams can replace the standard surgical knife, or scalpel, in some operations. Using a laser can reduce bleeding and damage to nearby healthy tissues.

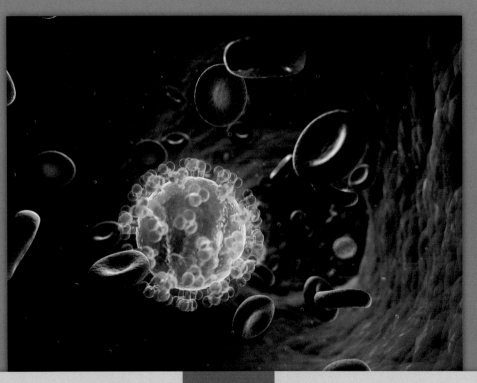

Scientists from several countries completed the Human Genome Project (started in 1990) to map the full set of genes in humans. This map allowed doctors to carry out genetic testing for such diseases as cancer. The full set of genes also helped researchers to develop new ways of replacing damaged genes.

1983   **2003**   **2007**

The human immunodeficiency virus (**HIV**) was first discovered. HIV damages the immune system, and can lead to acquired immune deficiency syndrome (**AIDS**), the final, life-threatening stages of the HIV infection. In 2006, the first single-dose pill was approved in the United States. This therapy stops the virus from causing damage and allows people with HIV to live longer.

Japanese and American scientists turned human skin cells into *stem cells*, which can transform into any kind of cell in the body.

As scientists work to eliminate such diseases as smallpox and polio, such new diseases as SARS, bird flu, and a difficult to treat infection known as MRSA, caused by staph bacteria, have appeared. Scientists are working on many new systems, including *gene therapy* (replacing faulty **genes** with healthy copies), that offer great promise for curing sickness. Some people worry that gene therapy could be used to change the basic nature of human beings by altering their genetic makeup. Powerful tools and new techniques require careful use and testing by trained researchers. As healthcare advances, new challenges will constantly arise for scientists and doctors to research within the field of medicine.

An outbreak of MERS (Middle East Respiratory Syndrome), a newly discovered viral illness, occurred in the Middle East.

The world's largest outbreak of deadly Ebola, a viral disease, occurred in Africa. The disease spread to other countries, including the United States, for the first time. By early 2016, more than 11,000 people had died of the disease.

2014-2016

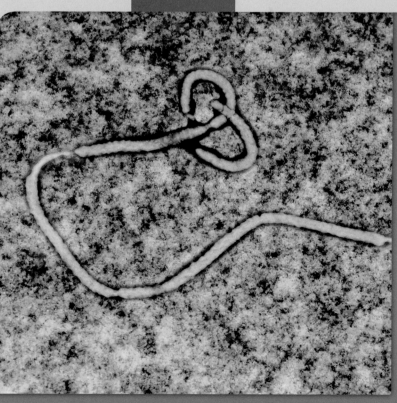

2012

2010

The Patient Protection and Affordable Care Act in the U.S. required individuals to buy private health insurance, but provided subsidies to the poor, to increase access to health care.

Glossary

anatomy the scientific study of the structure of human or animal bodies.

anesthesia a drug that makes a person unable to feel pain during medical treatment.

antibiotic a substance produced by some mold or bacteria that can destroy or prevent the growth of other bacteria and cells.

antiseptic a substance that prevents infection by stopping the growth of germs.

bacteria single-celled organisms that can only be seen using a microscope. Some bacteria cause disease.

cell the basic unit of life, of which all plants and animals are made.

DNA short for *deoxyribonucleic acid*; the chainlike structure found in cells that carries genetic information and passes on body features from parents to child.

epidemic an outbreak of disease that attacks many people at about the same time.

gene a part of a cell that determines which characteristics living things inherit from their parents.

germ a microorganism that causes disease. Germs include bacteria and viruses.

HIV short for *human immunodeficiency virus*; a virus that attacks certain white blood cells that are important to the immune system. People infected with HIV are unable to fight off infections. Without treatment, the HIV infection can become *acquired immune deficiency syndrome,* or **AIDS.**

heredity the process of passing genes from parents to child.

hormone a chemical substance produced in the body that encourages growth or influences how cells function.

hygiene methods that maintain health and prevent disease, such as cleanliness.

immune protected from disease.

inoculate to deliberately give a person a virus that causes a mild form of disease. This results in the person's **immunity** to the disease in the future.

Middle Ages the period in European history between ancient and modern times, from about the A.D. 400's through about the 1400's. The end date depends on the region of Europe considered.

midwife a person who helps women give birth.

Muslim a person who follows the religion of Islam.

Renaissance a great cultural movement that began in Italy during the early 1300's.

sanitation (n); sanitary (adj) the process of maintaining cleanliness to improve health conditions.

vaccination the process of giving a person a **vaccine,** a weakened form of a disease. The vaccine prevents or lessens the effects of that disease for a person in the future.

virus a microscopic living thing that causes infectious diseases.

X ray invisible rays that can pass through the skin and be used to produce pictures of bones and other internal body structures.

Find Out More

Books

The 12 Biggest Breakthroughs in Medicine by M. M. Eboch (12-Story Library, 2015)

Ancient Medical Technology: From Herbs to Scalpels by Michael Woods and Mary B. Woods (Twenty-First Century Books)

The Cold, Hard Facts About Science and Medicine in Colonial America by Elizabeth Raum (Capstone Press, 2012)

Discoveries in Medicine That Changed the World by Rose Johnson (Rosen Publishing, 2015)

The Greatest Doctor of Ancient Times: Hippocrates and His Oath by Mary Gow (Enslow Publishers, 2010)

Industrial Age Medicine by Rebecca Vickers (Raintree, 2012)

Medieval Medicine and Disease by Toney Allman (ReferencePoint Press, 2015)

Websites

BBC Two—Medicine Through Time
http://www.bbc.co.uk/programmes/b0077zf9/clips
Watch dozens of short videos that identify and discuss key moments in world medical history.

National Geographic Education – X-Rays Discovered
http://education.nationalgeographic.com/thisday/jan5/x-rays-discovered/
Learn about the discovery of X rays using National Geographic's Date in History feature.

New York Times - Milestones in Medical Technology
http://www.nytimes.com/interactive/2012/10/05/health/digital-doctor.html
Interact with a clickable timeline of medical history that includes images and facts surrounding important milestones.

PBS LearningMedia – The Discovery of Penicillin
http://www.pbslearningmedia.org/resource/odys08.sci.life.gen.discovery/the-discovery-of-penicillin/
How was penicillin discovered? Watch this PBS video to find out!

PBS NewsHour - How Elizabeth Blackwell Became the First Female Doctor in the U.S.
http://www.pbs.org/newshour/rundown/elizabeth-blackwell-becomes-the-first-woman-doctor-in-the-united-states/
Read an informational article on Elizabeth Blackwell's life as the first female doctor in the United States.

Science Museum – Brought to Life: Exploring the History of Medicine
http://www.sciencemuseum.org.uk/broughttolife/themes/science.aspx
Select from over a dozen topics on the medical field to get a greater look at the science behind the medical advances.

Index